The Mosaic Trail

Explorer Challenge

Find out what the red
bits make ...

OXFORD
UNIVERSITY PRESS

Chip had a book on Roman mosaics. "Look at this floor," he said. "It's a mosaic."

"It is made of lots of little bits," he said.
Just then, the key started to glow.

The key took them off.

It took them to a forest.
"How odd!" said Biff.

"I can see lots of little red bits," she said.

"They go on and on," said Chip.
"It's a trail."

"Can you hear that?" said Chip.
"It is a yell for help."

A man was stuck in a net.
"Set me free," he said.

"Robbers have run off with my wagon,"
he said. "I must get help!"

They ran to the top of the hill.
"Look! Romans on horses!" said Chip.

"Yell at them to get help," said the man.

The Romans got to the top of the hill.

"Robbers took my wagon," said the man. "They took the sacks of bits for the mosaic floor."

"Jump up," said a Roman.
"The wagon cannot be far off."

15

They soon got to
the wagon.

"This sack is torn," said Chip. "It was spilling the bits."

"We can help pick the bits up,"
said Biff.

"Thank you," said the man.
"This is the plan for the mosaic floor."

"It's fantastic," said Chip.
The key started to glow.

20

Biff had some little bits of mosaic.
"I have six bits," she said. "But we will need
lots for a mosaic."

Retell the Story

Look at the pictures and retell the story in your own words.

Look Back, Explorers

Why were there red bits on the ground?

What were the bits for?

Imagine you are talking to the man who was making the mosaic floor. What questions would you ask him?

Chip says that the mosaic floor is *fantastic*. What other words can you think of that mean the same as *fantastic*?

Did you find out what the red bits made?

Explorer Challenge: the cock's comb in the mosaic floor (page 20)

23

What's Next, Explorers?

Now that you've read about the Roman mosaic Biff and Chip saw, you can find out about other mosaics …

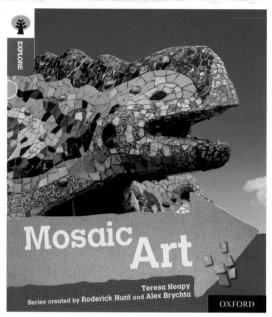

Explorer Challenge
for *Mosaic Art*

Find out how many steps there are …